# Advance

# Excel

# Essentials

By

David K. Ewen, M.Ed.

# Advance Excel Essentials

# By:  David K. Ewen, M.Ed.

ISBN-13: 978-1500432898

ISBN-10: 150043289X

# Advance Excel Essentials

By

David K. Ewen, M.Ed.

## About the author:

David K. Ewen, M.Ed. is a professor, author, speaker, talk show host, film producer, and publisher. He is the founder of Ewen Prime Company and has been in media production since 1994. In 2004, he founded Forest Academy and has toured the seven states of New York and New England on entrepreneurial studies. David is a consulting professor at the Saylor Academy in Washington, D.C. and linguistics professor in Tokyo, Japan.

## About the book:

Advance Excel Essentials is the second part of Excel Essentials by David K. Ewen, M.Ed.

# Printing to Fit

- **TAB**:                      Page Layout
- **SECTION**:            Scale to Fit

## SCALE TO FIT
- Width – Set to automatic to match Height setting or 1, 2, 3, etc. pages
- Height – Set to automatic to match Width setting or 1, 2, 3, etc. pages

## PAGE BREAKS
- Click Breaks

# Hide ROWS   and / or   COLUMNS

- Highlight the labels for ROWS (B, C, D, etc.)   and rows (1, 2, 3, etc)

- Right Click – Click Hide and later you can click unhide

# Error Message

**Error**    **Meaning**

**#DIV/0!**    Trying to divide by 0

**#N/A!**    A formula or a function inside a formula cannot find the referenced data

**#NAME?**    Text in the formula is not recognized

**#NULL!**    A space was used in formulas that reference multiple ranges; a comma separates range references. Error message occurs when the two or more cell references are not separated correctly in a formula.

**#NUM!**    A formula has invalid numeric data for the type of operation

**#REF!**    A reference is invalid. An invalid cell reference error message occurs when a spreadsheet formula contains incorrect cell references.

**#VALUE!**    The wrong type of operand or function argument is used

# Formulas

- SUM          Calculates the sum of a group of values

- AVERAGE      Calculates the mean of a group of values

- COUNT        Counts the number of cells in a range that contains numbers

- INT          Removes the decimal portion of a number, leaving just the integer portion

- ROUND        Rounds a number to a specified number of decimal places or digit positions

- IF           Tests for a true or false condition and then returns one value or another

- NOW          Returns the system date and time

- TODAY        Returns the system date, without the time

- SUMIF        Calculates a sum from a group of values, but just of values that are included
  because a condition is met

- COUNTIF      Counts the number of cells in a range that match a criteria

ADDITION cell A1 to A10 = sum (A1: A10)
AVERAGE cell A1 to A10 = average (A1: A10)
MAXIMUM cell A1 to A10 = max (A1: A10)
MINIMUM cell A1 to A10 = min (A1: A10)

Conditional: =IF (condition; value "if true"; value "otherwise")
Example:     =IF(A1 <= 0; "ordering", "stock")

# Data Validation

- Select Data from the Tool Bar
- Select Data Tool Section from the Data Ribbon
- Select Data Validation
- The cells affected are the ones highlighted

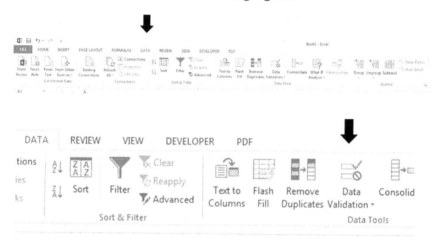

Data
Validation ▾

- <u>Setting</u>:  Validation Criteria

- <u>Input Message</u>:  Instructions when cell is highlighted

- <u>Error Alert</u>:  Instructions when wrong information is entered

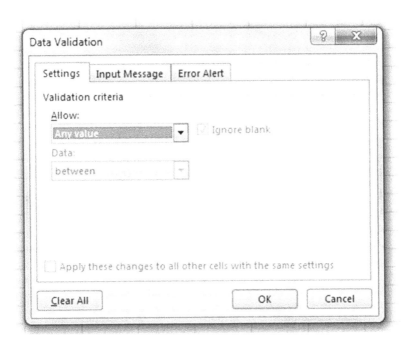

# Filter Data (Data Filtering)

Filtering of data with column
headers over a table of data is done
by:
Highlight Columns
- Select DATA tab
- Go to Sort & Filter Section
- Click Filter (picture of funnel)

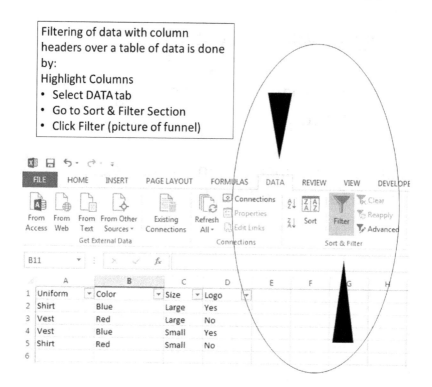

With the drop down arrow, you can filter a search
using masking characters * and ?

You can set up a control key function like **CTRL-a** to
perform a routinely used set of filter criteria.    This is
done through a Macro.   See section on Macros

# Locking Individual Cells

The default setting to locking cells on a worksheet is ALL cells are locked.    A step
needs to be done to make sure individual cells can be unlocked.

- All cells are highlighted
- Select PROTECTION tab in FORMAT CELLS
- Uncheck the Locked check box (clear the check)

**Click here to select all cells on
sheet and right click --- Select
Format Cells**

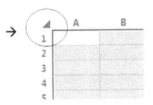

**Select**
←
**Format Cells**

Another way to get to the above screen is to click here from the FONT section of the HOME tab ←

Next ...

- Highlight the cells that need to be locked
- Go back and check the LOCKED check box from the Protection tab in Format

- Now go to REVIEW tab on main ribbon and go to CHANGES section
- Use this to lock the sheet – only the defined locked cells will be locked

# Share Workbook

You can share a workbook on a server so that it can be accessed by multiple users.

- Click the **Review** tab.
- Select the **Changes** group.
- Click **Share Workbook**.

# Formula Investigation & Fixing

- <u>Formulas</u> tab from main ribbon
- <u>Formula Auditing</u> section

- FORMULAS → Formula Auditing

Trace Precedents     Show Formulas

Trace Dependents     Error Checking ▾

Remove Arrows ▾ (fx) Evaluate Formula

Formula Auditing

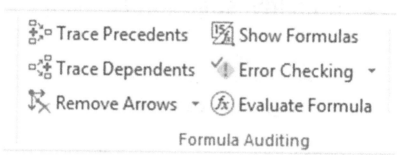

Formula Auditing

## PRECEDENTS & DEPENDENTS

Arrows are drawn showing each cell's precedents and dependents when you click

- Trace Precedents
- Trace Dependents

When you want to clear arrows, click Remove Arrows

## SHOW FORMULAS
The formula values can be shown in the cell for easy recognition of the cell function.

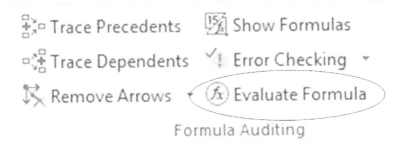

Trace Precedents    Show Formulas

Trace Dependents    Error Checking

Remove Arrows    (fx) Evaluate Formula

Formula Auditing

Enter the following:
• A1:  1   (the number 1)
• B1:  =((A1+2)*3)/4     (value displayed is 2.25)

Highlight B1 and click Evaluate Formula
Click Evaluate,  Click it again,  Formula operation is
show step-by-step

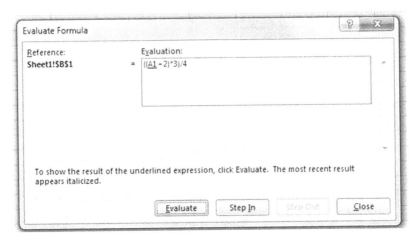

Enter the following:

- A1:  set value as the number 1
- B1:  Set the value as  the formula **=A1 / 0**

You will see that B1 says #DIV/0! .  You can't divide by zero. This is an error message.  Let's pretend you didn't know what that was and need help solving the formula problem.

- Go to **Formulas** Tab
- Go to **Formula Auditing** section
- Click **Error Checking** button
    - Check error
    - Trace error

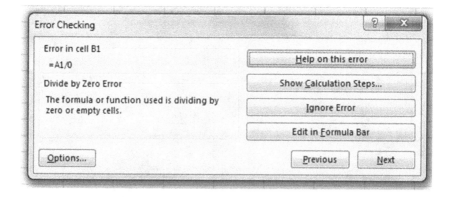

Use the "Watch Window" to track cell values and associated formulas.   Use this as part of formula auditing.

# Naming Cells

You can give cells a name.  For example A1 can be called APPLE
- Highlight Cell A1
- Go to FORMULAS tab
- Go to DEFINED NAMES section
- Click DEFINE NAME

You can name a single cell or multiple cells. Cells can have more than one name.

Two groups of cells being defined under a name can overlap.

# Using Variables

You can give cells a name.  For example A1 can be called APPLE
- Highlight Cell A1
- Go to FORMULAS tab
- Go to DEFINED NAMES section
- Click DEFINE NAME

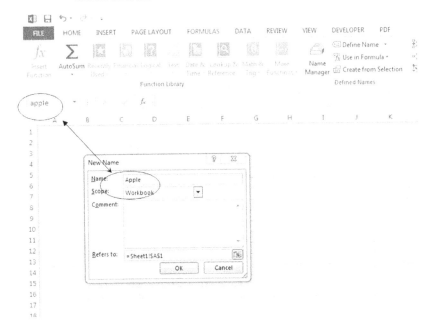

## You can use defined variables in formulas

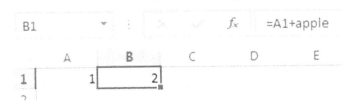

You can define a group of cells under one name

Example A1:E1 is called Range

# Macros

## (1) Select VIEW

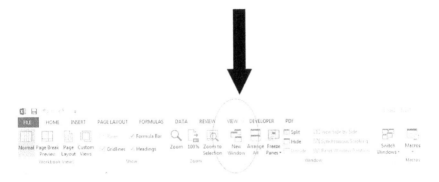

## (2) Select Macros

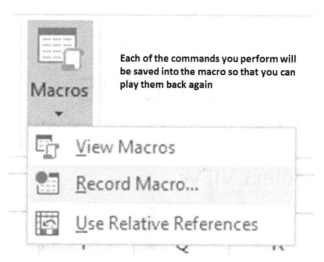

Each of the commands you perform will be saved into the macro so that you can play them back again

- Select VIEW from Ribbon
- Select Record macro

------------------------------------------------------------

- Select name of Macro
- Indicate shortcut key to initiate macro
- Store Macro in: This Workbook
- Description – Entered detailed description

After performing commands, click Macros and select Stop Recording

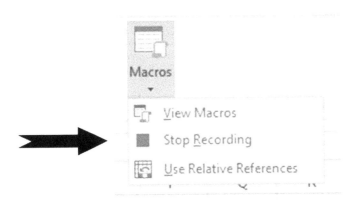

Execute Macro by selecting CTRL and programmed key  CTRL-a

## Example of Recording a Macro

Before recording, put a number with a 3 decimal places, example 12.345

### Start recording macro  (set keyboard ctrl-a)

- Change # of decimal places of **A1** to **2**
- Change so number has dollar sign
- Change font
    - Size bigger (and  make column wider)
    - Bold
    - Italic
    - Red
    - Underline
    - New font type

### Stop recording macro

### Test macro (execute ctrl-b)

- Go to A5 and enter number 56.789.
- Execute Macro

# Editing a Macro

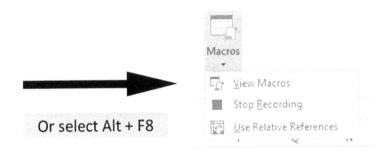

Or select Alt + F8

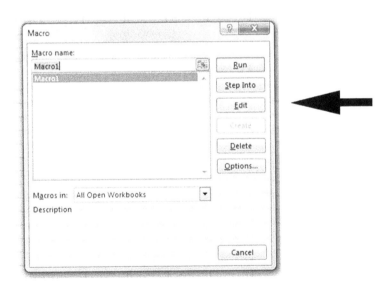

# Edit Macro (Example) – Change Font Size

# Close & Test when done

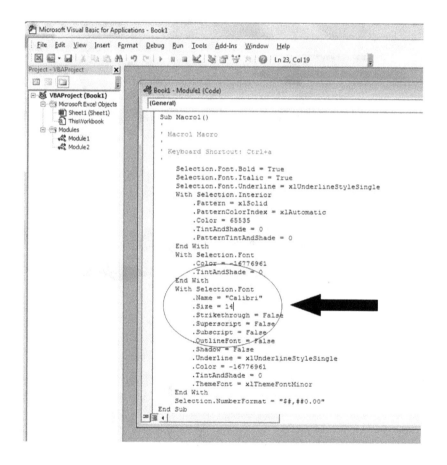

## Exercise:

## Create a Macro with Data Filtering

## Record Macro:
### Setting filters

# Tools for Macro (Advance)

If you don't see the DEVELOPER tab, then you must add it.

FILE > OPTIONS > CUSTOMIZED RIBBON

- In the very far left menu bar, select "**Customize Ribbon**"
- In the upper right make sure the drop down selection is "**Main Tabs**"
- Put a check mark next to "**Developer**"

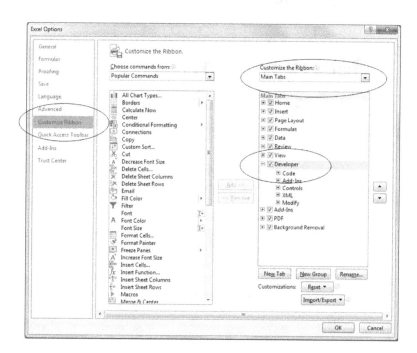

# Visual Basic for Excel Macros
# VBA: Visual Basic for Applications

http://www.excel-easy.com/vba.html

http://www.easyexcelvba.com

http://vb.wikia.com

# Create New Macro

Click
Create
Here

**Enter
any
name
here**

```
Dim i As Integer

For i = 1 To 6

    Cells(i, 1).Value = 100

Next i
```

Enter this code below

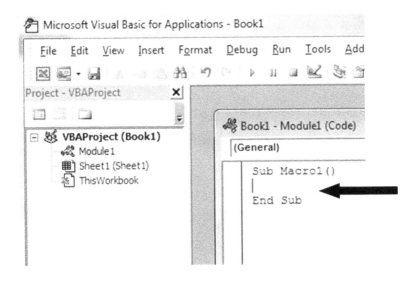

# Create Macro Shortcut Key

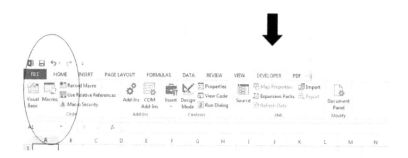

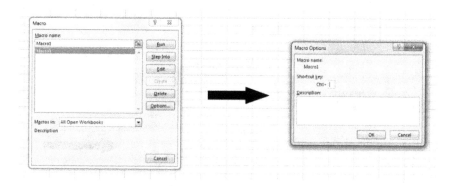

- Select Developer
- Select Macro
- Select Options
- Create Shortcut

# Visual Basic Loops

### Column A1 to A6 has value of 100

```
Dim i As Integer

For i = 1 To 6
   Cells(i, 1).Value = 100
Next i
```

----------------------------------------------------------

### Column A1-A6 & B1-B6  has value of 100

```
Dim i As Integer, j As Integer

For i = 1 To 6
   For j = 1 To 2
      Cells(i, j).Value = 100
   Next j
Next i
```

------------------------------------------------

### A1 to A5 has value of 20

```
Dim i As Integer
i = 1

Do While i < 6
   Cells(i, 1).Value = 20
   i = i + 1
Loop
```

-----------------------------------------------------
### (START WITH: enter numbers in first six cells of column 1
### This macro adds 10 to column 1 and puts result in column 2

```
Dim i As Integer
i = 1

Do While Cells(i, 1).Value <> ""
   Cells(i, 2).Value = Cells(i, 1).Value + 10
   i = i + 1
Loop
```

## Assign a value to variable Greeting from cell B3 and then paste in B6:F1

Dim Greeting As String

Greeting = Range("B3")
Range("B6:F14") = Greeting

## Assign the value Hello to the variable Greeting

Dim Greeting As String

Greeting = "Hello"
Range("B6:F14") = Greeting

# Mail Merge

Older versions of WORD start mail merge like this:

On the **Tools** menu, point to **Letters and Mailings**, and then click **Mail Merge**

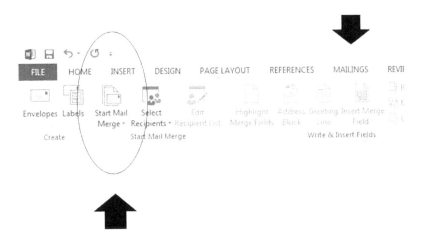

**Select Letters or type of document**

## Selecting Recipients

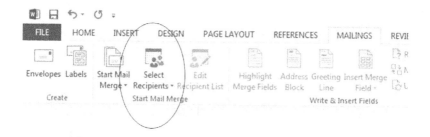

## Select the option to create a new list that is saved as MS-Access. You can also use an existing list from Excel

If using Excel to create address book, create a sheet with the following headers:

- Title
- First Name
- Last Name
- Company Name
- Address Line 1
- Address Line 2
- City
- State
- ZIP Code
- Country or Region
- Home Phone
- Work Phone
- E-mail Address

# REFERENCES MAILINGS

## Address Greeting Insert Merge
## Block Line Field ▾

### Write & Insert Fields

**Click to add Address at top, Greeting line near the top after the address, then certain fields like person's first name if referenced in the middle of the letter.**

# Thank you.

## Advance Excel Essentials

By: David K. Ewen, M.Ed.

Copyright © 2014, Ewen Prime Company

www.ingramcontent.com/pod-product-compliance
Lightning Source LLC
Chambersburg PA
CBHW060933050326
40689CB00013B/3073